A gift for:

From:

Published by Hallmark Gift Books,
a division of Hallmark Cards, Inc.,
Kansas City, MO 64141
Visit us on the Web at www.Hallmark.com.

Editor: Megan Langford
Art Director: Kevin Swanson
Designer: Rob Latimer
Production Designer: Bryan Ring

ISBN: 978-1-59530-270-0

GGT1225

Printed and bound in China
DEC11

GIFT BOOKS

Congrats, GRAD!

Wisdom and Inspiration
to Celebrate Your Success

Do you dare to live as the superstar you were meant to be?

Say yes.

dre

*Whatever you do or dream
you can, begin it.
Boldness has genius, power,
and magic in it.*

— JOHANN WOLFGANG VON GOETHE

A single dream can launch
the journey of a lifetime.

As soon as we
left the ground,
I knew I had to fly.

— AMELIA EARHART

Every day
is a wonderful
chance to be
what you've
dreamed . . .
to do what
you've
imagined.

KEEP ON DREAMING, KEEP O

EACHING, KEEP ON ACHIEVING.

When it is dark enough, you can see the stars.

— RALPH WALDO EMERSON

DREAM BIG. BE HAPPY.

Never compromise
on the things that
really matter to you.

So many of our dreams
at first seem impossible,
then they seem improbable,
and then, when we
summon the will, they soon
become inevitable.

— CHRISTOPHER REEVE

DREAMS take time, patience, sustained effort, and a willingness to fail if they are ever to be anything more than dreams.

NO DREAM
IS BEYOND
YOUR
REACH.

Dream
no small
dreams.

— VICTOR HUGO

You see things;
and you say, "Why?"
But I dream things
that never were;
and I say, "Why not?"

— GEORGE BERNARD SHAW

beli

Achievement begins with BELIEF.

The future belongs
to those who believe
in the beauty of
their dreams.

— ELEANOR ROOSEVELT

One person with passion is better than 40 who are merely interested.

— TOM CONNELLAN

Your future doesn't lie ahead of you, waiting to happen. It lies deep inside of you, waiting to be discovered.

Attitude is the master key to life's little locks.

Whether you
think you can
or think you can't,
you're right.

— HENRY FORD

My spirit takes flight.
I am fearless and free—
to explore,

to express, to begin . . . to be me.

Make a fresh start. Blaze a new trail.
Walk in the footsteps of your own dreams.

Courage is its own reward.

— PLAUTUS

It's kind of fun to do the impossible.

— WALT DISNEY

Embrace your dreams with passion!

Those that don't got it,
can't show it.
Those that got it,
can't hide it.

— ZORA NEALE HURSTON

Your future can be decided
in two easy steps:

1. Find your dream.
2. Chase it.

All you need
in this life
is ignorance
and confidence,
and then
success is sure.

— MARK TWAIN

The world
is a blank
canvas, and
your life
is a
masterpiece
waiting
to happen.

YOUR LIFE

Life is more interesting if
you don't have all the answers.

The question isn't who is going to let me; it's who is going to stop me.

– AYN RAND

To dream the impossible dream is to begin making it possible.

Nobody else's footsteps lead exactly where you're going

Every calling is great when greatly pursued.

— OLIVER WENDELL HOLMES

It's better to look ahead and prepare than to look back and regret.

This is your life—
　　make it what you want it to be.

Experience is
the name everyone
gives to their
mistakes.

— OSCAR WILDE

CLASS OF 2

The important thing is not to stop questioning.

— ALBERT EINSTEIN

Sometimes all that stands between you and the ride of a lifetime is simply getting in the saddle and seeing what you're made of.

One doesn't discover new lands without consenting to lose sight of the shore for a very long time.

— ANDRÉ GIDE

There are only two ways to live your life. One is as though nothing is a miracle. The other is as though everything is a miracle.

— ALBERT EINSTEIN

Nothing in the world can take the place of persistence.

— CALVIN COOLIDGE

Remember, while traveling the road to success, it's fun to get a little lost along the way.

Obstacles cannot crush me. Every obstacle yields to stern resolve. He who is fixed to a star does not change his mind.

— LEONARDO DA VINCI

achieve.

It's good to know life has a lot to offer you, but even better to know that you have a lot to offer life!

The
best
thing
about
the
future
is
that
it
comes
only
one
day
at
a
time.

— ABRAHAM LINCOLN

Glory gives herself
only to those who have
always dreamed of her.

— CHARLES DE GAULLE

Small opportunities are often the beginning of great enterprises.

— DEMOSTHENES

Through hard work and ambition, the brightest dreams come true.

Success is how high
you bounce when
you hit bottom.

— GENERAL GEORGE S. PATTON

Success is often
just an idea away.

— FRANK TYGER

Love what you do . . .
Do what you love.

Act as if it were
impossible to fail.

— DOROTHEA BRANDE

When you can do the common things of life in an uncommon way, you will command the attention of the world.

— GEORGE WASHINGTON CARVER

Graduation is the bridge that connects years of learning to a lifetime of success and happiness.

No one ever attains
very eminent success
by simply doing what
is required of him.

— CHARLES KENDALL ADAMS

Eighty percent of
success is showing up.

— WOODY ALLEN

The only way to live happily ever after is to do it one day at a time.

Just because something doesn't do what you planned it to do doesn't mean it's useless.

— THOMAS ALVA EDISON

One of life's great
rules is this:
The more you give,
the more you get.

— WILLIAM H. DANFORTH

Cherish your yesterdays, dream your tomorrows, but live your todays. Tomorrow belongs to those who fully use today.

Be who you are.
Do what you love.
Make a difference.
CHANGE THE WORLD.

It is never too late
to be what you
might have been.

— GEORGE ELIOT

Never, never, never, never give up.

— WINSTON CHURCHILL

My life is my message.

— MAHATMA GANDHI

Do not let what you
cannot do interfere
with what you can do.

— JOHN WOODEN

Maybe good things come to those who wait, but the best things come to those who seize the moment and make it their own.

CLASS OF 2

Nothing great
was ever achieved
without enthusiasm.

— RALPH WALDO EMERSON

Horizons are made for going BEYOND.

Happiness is mainly attitude, and love is a way of life. Knowing this, you can't go wrong.

If you have built castles in the air,
your work need not be lost;
that is where they should be.
Now put the foundations under them.

— HENRY DAVID THOREAU

Life is a work in progress.

Today you're seeing a dream come true, but this is just the start of many dreams.

If you have enjoyed this book,
we would love to hear from you.

Please send your comments to:
Hallmark Book Feedback
P.O. Box 419034, Mail Drop 215
Kansas City, MO 64141

Or e-mail us at:
booknotes@hallmark.com